"FINDING
MY
NATIVE TONGUE"
(WHO AM I?)

AUTHOR BIO

I'm Arbria Owens, a daughter of the most high. I am an esthetician in the Las Vegas community, helping others take care of themselves with skincare and beauty. Most importantly that true beauty that comes from within. I am from Fresno, CA and moved to Vegas when I was a teen.

This is my first book as an author and a collection of poetry. I fell in love with poetry when I was in high school. Learning and reading about different literature spoke to me. Literature ignited a flame, and I'm here to introduce you to …

"Finding my Native Tongue".

BOOK DESCRIPTION

Finding My Native Tongue is a collection of Poetry that will take you on a journey. This journey was about finding my identity and purpose and how we go through different seasons. Sometimes, we let our past, relationships and the things we do define us. You will discover that this is not true. May this book be a blessing to you, amen

DEDICATION PAGE

I want to honor and give glory to my Abba, my King, and my God. . Without him, this wouldn't have been possible. I love you!

I want to give thanks to my family, my heart Joshua And my friends who supported me and believed in my vision.

I want to give thanks and love to my church Refreshing Waters Ministries, for planting a seed. Thank you for being my family, for being a Training ground for the kingdom and always building and supporting me.

Last I would love to give thanks to Deona Braxton for being a great mentor and help birth this creation.

TABLE OF CONTENTS

SUMMER THE SEEK

Have you ever had a desire to search beyond what we were told? Yes, I do. I have a thirst for understanding, I want to have joy but most of all the truth. Looking for truth in life, relationships, love, and experiences can be tricky. I was never the person who took the time to discover who I am. I just let what happened to my life define who I was. I took all my pain, my hurt, my anger and what the world said I was as my identity. Deep within, I knew I was more than what I was told. I didn't know how to activate what was in me. It took a traumatic event to shake me up and lead me out of the hole I was in. I needed answers and the chance to seek and find them. What I didn't know was that this journey was going to take me to some roads that I had to face.

Discovery, I am ready to let you take your course.

THE SEARCH

I ride the pavement to discover what roadways lay ahead.

Each passage is an adventure I want to pursue.

I don't care where I start!

I know in the end I will meet my purpose.

Truth, wisdom, and identity.

I'm ready to meet your mountain tops.

Once I encounter all of you.

I will be ready to spot the other side.

YOU

I want to love you with all my might, but I don't know how to.

I don't even know how to love myself completely.

I am told to love the creator with everything that I have, He will show me
the way.

First I have to let him unlock every door.

That's the price that I have to pay.

You all might think this is easy.

For you, it's easy, for me, it's like a snake on the tree waiting for the perfect
moment to strike its prey.

I will be forced to face myself.

I'm not sure if I'll ever be ready.

Unlocking those doors will bring forth freedom, and I can finally meet who
I'm meant to be.

Pulling up the covers is what frightens me.

I don't know who I would see.

What if,

Who I'm supposed to be is not who I thought I was going to be?

And in the end, I am not me.

See, this is why I hide in the clouds, only letting the river kiss my toes.

My spirit says let the current take me.

My outer shell tells me to stay, and see where the river flows.

I listened to the outside when it comes to you.

I don't want to be swept away.

I know your river will lead me to a grotto of Paradise.

You favor me, and I adore that.

But the taste of uncertainty is ruling my desire to float.

SAILING

Love, sometimes trying to understand you is like trying to touch the bottom of the ocean. The deeper you go, the darker it gets and the more pressure that is upon you.

It's easy to become absent in your waves.

You can swallow anything up.

I love how you are so mysterious. Even though you bring danger, you're worth searching.

Ships sail your body looking for treasures and the clear waters.

VOICE

I open my mouth, but you only see my lips move.

The shaking of my cord is moving to produce the sound of silence. I know I'm a little girl and I should not speak. This little girl will be big one day, so understand.

My soul left me when I didn't know what was true. You didn't know that your little girl was gone. Time flew by and identity mistaken, I was the road that everyone had taken.

I cry; I sob until my eyes were bloody red.

Your little girl laid in the closet or under the bed, looking at the dark spaces and wanted to be dead.

Invisible I was, invisible I accepted. I walked my years hidden.

I was wearing a disguise to the character that I needed to be. Really I just wanted someone, mostly you to see.

Taunt, shame and shun in a cage. When you didn't come in time, I build up in rage.

I wanted you to free me!

Trust has perished. How can I ask for help?

You didn't even reach out your hand if you did, it disappeared.

I wanted and yearned for you to be near.

Wondering how to protect, be secure and stable.

Not knowing if I'm able.

I'm trapped and lost in this house of horror.

Bodies I pleased, bodies, I let them take me, not understanding my worth.

Those bodies did not care, they left me in the dirt.

Hands grabbed me, my eyes were filled in fear. I thank the Lord that I am still here.

I'm ashamed of the murky puddle I rolled into.

Can I really blame myself?

I was still gone on autopilot through this life.

By now I didn't know who or what was nice.

I got led to a tunnel, were creatures accepted me. I was deceived by the lie they displayed.

I had no chance of freedom. Now I speak, and my lips are still not moving.

I am saved, loved and okay. So I am going to keep doing what I am doing and will go my way.

Holes are being filled with love from the refreshing waters of above.

I love you so much!! Even though there is smoke in between us.

I just want your love if you know what I mean.

I'm growing into a lady that you don't understand.

Please get to know me so I can get to know you.

Then we can stand, we are no longer strangers with hurt in our hands.

This is not a finger force in the eyes. I don't want you to be blind.

This little girl is a lady now as I once said. This little girl wants to live and not be dead.

This living being is free! It's true, but I want to be free and have you.

This little girl has spoken to be heard and now she can sleep.

This little girl is not broken anymore and now is at peace.

PROVE AND PUSH

Loyalty, compassion, humbleness, and love is what I seek.

I feel it all the time, and I know it is apart of me.

My heart throbs, and sometimes I can't breathe because all the pain and suffering that is always around me.

Most of the time I feel it within myself.

Am I ever good enough, Am I ever good enough, Work harder, Be smarter, Go for it? Don't hold back.

Push push push! Run faster, Dress better. Get a better job.

Just go, Just go, Just go,

Don't stop or you will fail.

Who do you think you are? You Obey me!

In a quick second, I've become a slave, and my wrists are bruised because of the heavy metal I blindly choose. Dust, Fog, and Coal in my lungs I gasp for air.

I breathe I feel no relief.

HELP ME!! HELP ME!! I scream you guys can't see!

As I fall to the ground broken, I feel comfort and discover that I need to only try for the one that is the truth.

To you I scare to you I might intimidate.

I don't want too, I just choose to love than to hate.

You need space no pressure, don't want no one or nobody telling you what to do.

I'm sorry, I'm sorry I just believe in all of you.

My mouth is harsh, my presence is unfair please don't take the pain out on my love that is not there.

I am not perfect; I am human too. I'm learning to take back steps to correct my wrongs and see my dreams come through.

The path I walk some might not understand.

I walk because I need to and want to be a better man.

Daughter, Daughter I am for the one above, my eyes are renewed and restored because I am loved.

Please! Please! Please, don't throw your sticks and stones at me.

In the end, I will always love you all to the depths of the deep sea.

Faith! Faith! Has brought me to my knees, you see weakness, I see strength, love, and mercy to defeat my enemies.

Fire! Fire!! That roars inside my metal chains, have finally broken and died

I'M FREE!! I'M FREE!!! You finally see no more prove and push you are forever deceased.......

WOUNDS

I look in the mirror, and I see bruises, blood, and holes.

No matter how many times I patch up my injuries, they will not heal.

Where is the antidote or the doctor for this situation!

I've looked high and low.

Time is having its effect on me.

Epiphany strikes,

I've been looking in the wrong places.

With the remaining strength I have left, I am guided to the author.

My eyes widen like a long-eared owl.

It's a book of love letters and promises.

The surgery tools.

I found the answer.

Fall the Fullness

Yes, I made it!! I had a goal and was determined to fulfill it. We all know that feeling when we are on the right path to achieve a task. You feel so great that you have overcomed the minor tribulations. You want to see your accomplishments birthed instantly. Promises have been spoken over you, and you want to jump into your purpose without growth.

You are ready now to share to the world your story, and what you have been going through. I knew that this is where I am supposed to be in my life. I was okay with where I was at.

My relationship was great. I knew that my relationship would grow and in time there will be no need for any more effort because we were good with what we had. My spiritual life was good too. I was forming a relationship with God and was a part of my church, and that was enough. I thought I was ready to pour out to others. My business was starting, and it was blooming. I was going places. I got blinded by the image of making it. My thoughts are, all I have to do is keep things here, and I will be happy. What I didn't realize was that I was settling. God had more for me, and it was time to trust him.

All these great things were happening, with all honesty it was only the beginning. I still don't know who I am and God's work is still in progress.

Discovery is unfolding.

13

No Hiding

Attention! Attention here me now,

I'm speaking to all of you.

It is a time to feel, it is a time to deal, it is a time to be real, it is the time to heal.

We can't continue to move this way running through life like we are okay.

Choosing a mask, of the day like we are the performer ready and set to take the stage.

Eventually, we will run out of the room. We can't keep moving or changing locations because our houses are getting full.

We say there is no hope or people never change.

To be honest, everyone is hurt, and we all are playing the same game.

It is scary because when the truth comes, sometimes there is doubt, wondering if we made the right decision to open up that door that leads to all our affliction.

We are going to war with ourselves because we want to be different.

It's not about being different; it's about accepting the beatings, Lash, gashes, bruises, and damages that has been done, even if we don't see that there is one.

One who see us like this.

We are so precious to Him you all see, He gave his precious son who is dear to him for you and me.

The door that is now open seams to tell us that there is no light, that's a lie, because the light is the one who is by our side.

With every tear, every breathe, every battle, and when we feel blind and not knowing where we are going;

He has our hand leading us through it all, and don't worry about the fall because He will pick us up and carry us after all.

Walking through many halls, we understand that we had to face us.

It's not just people,

It's us as well.

We won't see the change instantly.

We have to be vulnerable, consistent, and willing to dwell.

Then we will be discharged, delivered and released.

We will then have the joy that we seek.

We will look back and see that in time we had slain the beast.

PAGES

Flip me until you are tired.

Your heart wants more, but your mind and hands needs rest.

Trying to research me won't tell you the truth.

Lines states the facts

But my pages don't define who I am.

You would only take your own perspective.

The clue is a relationship

FORGIVE

Forgiveness can only be given and not lent.

To mask the flaw, will only leave you damage with a dent.

Holding on to that grudge will make you suffer and bend.

You are in a bed, asking death for a lend.

Knowing better and regretting now that you shouldn't have waited until the
end.

Only you can take the blame.

You are the one who is being lame.

Letting foolishness stop you from your aim,

To be at peace and take your place in Heaven as your claim.

You let the enemy play you like a card game.

Dang. That's a shame.

Now is the chance to release

The chance to be at ease.

A chance to live.

A chance to give.

Not being bitter, but being vivid .

FORMATION

Bubbling up I want to dash forward.

I am making time my enemy.

I'm filled and need to pour out.

I am learning how not to be only dry or to be only full.

Balance is what I am always getting into a tussle with.

Growing takes being a child, the will needs to be there and sending pride out
the window.

Building is occurring

I need to form a pact with the process

Then the skyscraper I will be.

MACHINES

To feed it is important, To nourish and care for it, like your newborn child is the task.

You love it, and it's yours to keep until it is time for it to go home.

At first, you're cautious with it and want to keep it safe. You hold on to it for your dear life.

As it changes you become more reckless with it, consuming whatever, whoever and anything you please to it.

Running it down until it is worn out.

Stop!

Why did you take it to the point of brokenness?

You realize that you can't waste it.

If you do, you will break it.

It's all that you have.

Clarity kicks in.

You take it and clean it. You are rebuilding the pieces back together making it better than it was before.

20

It is now your temple that you honor and cherish.

You know that it is sacred.

LAND & WATER

The sun kisses your mountain tops.

The wind shakes your trees.

I watch from afar and want you to be close to me.

I admire your groundedness, you can be still with peace, your forest is an adventure I want to roam and seek, it's too hard for me to explore because I am out of reach.

I love you.

My waves soar high when one of your charming critters says hi.

At last, you tell me you love me, and I am sold, we finally touched at our threshold.

Calm, swift, a strong moving force you are there to greet when my current is out of control, you are always there to comfort me.

I cause sometimes raging storms, and you fight to take cover.

Even when I'm a whirlwind and not at my best, you are still a great lover.

Our brightest days are great, we create a marvelous place, an atmosphere to celebrate.

You are my Land King, and I am your Ocean Queen. We are different and come from two different worlds as it seems.

Everything about us, we create the perfect dream.

IDEAS

Ideas and ideas forming inside

Ideas that wants to come alive.

There are so many, which one do I plant first.

My thoughts are overflowing, and I just need to let them out.

If I keep letting my seeds randomly fall out,

I will suffer and cause them not to sprout.

The wind shift and a voice say to stay on the good ground.

With patience, nourishing, and my time

You will reap a good harvest.

Fly Away

I look up to the sun and feel its rays beam on my cheeks.

I look down, and I'm back to where I was.

Reality is here, but I want to be there.

My wings are stuck. I cry; I plea, I really want to go up and fly to be free.

A place where I can soar, then deal and heal with my pain in a mighty roar.

The clicking noise told me to be, then I would finally see.

My thoughts pounder to understand.

Running around in my head.

Thinking and thinking, pounding beats; my cheeks become stain with my tears because I don't know what I am told, means.

A path forms for me to explore it, I have to go I can't ignore it.

I walk the path that leads to an edge.

I stop and freeze, only to see there is no going back.

At that moment I discover it is faith that I lack.

I close my eyes and breathe.

I jumped and feel myself falling. I opened my eyes. I'm really flying.

The skies are beautiful, and their mysteries intrigued me, I understand it is FAITH that freed me.

I'm dancing with the sun, no longer a dream.

Its rays wave to me to say hello, and it tells me that I was always high and not below.

At that moment, I had taken a chance to be. I now know that I am and that I have always been the key.

WINTER THE HUNGER

I'm dried out and hopeless at this point. Did I make the right move? Am I doing this right? The questions I would ask myself because of the doubt. My past is affecting me now. This time I can't hide or run from it anymore. I have the choice to back out or to stay. This process we all don't like. When it gets hard, we want to leave and quit. I thought I became the winner. I was oppressed by depression, I was oppressed by a lot of things. I fought and won the battle, but I didn't win the war. I still let hurt get the best me. Feeling unworthy and didn't understand who God wanted me to be or who He created me to be. If I stay true, then I will have to endure it all. I wanted to do right for others, for those who I care for and most of all Him . People pleasing Is what I struggled with. I doubted my relationship with my partner and felt like he and no one else didn't know me or could see me suffering. Then I became angry and frustrated because my natural characteristics cause me this pain. People I loved went away. They hurt my heart. How am I supposed to trust, love and give, if I will forever be the doormat? During all of this, I'm broken and weak. I'm hungry begging for the Lord to feed me and give me the tools I need to move on.

My God showed me alright. I was so blinded because I was doing everything wrong. He loves me and told me He was there, but I wasn't allowing him to be there for me. I kept trying to do things out of my own strength. Then

27

eventually I was worn out. There was nothing left in me, and it was time to start depending on God. Once I had let go and let all the weakness show, it allowed me to be light and free from trauma and pain. That's when he came in and gave me the strength to be stronger than a thousand giants. I never had to do it on my own. I needed to give God full control so he can fully heal the holes, wounds, and destruction that was inside of me. Wisdom fell upon me, with him I would win the battle and the war.

Discovery is transformation

PICTURE

Beautifully laying on this granite wall ready for the world to see.

Different eyes admire my fine strokes of colors.

They wonder how did I come to be, then they go back to where they were.

I hang up high and listen to their whispers and chatters. Each one is about something different. I get a bump by this soft, warm thing, and I now have a dent. Days go by, the chatters and the whispers seem not to notice.

I feel it, today is the day that I'm going to get a fix.

I'll be back to my beautiful self. The dent is gone,

It's time to get back to my home.

Before I leave, I sit and wait, then splash, I'm wet!

I'm leaking!

I'm definitely not the same anymore.

I go into a workshop, and different brushes come and try to restore what was once there.

Now It's time to go back home.

I pass by a shimmery glass and see my reflection, I see, and I am not the same. Would anyone even notice?

I am back home laying against the granite wall.

Familiar stretched holes, and wide eyes are in my face.

I wonder if they missed me.

With confusion, they do not know it's me. Am I that different now? With a broken heart, I just hang not knowing what is to come.

FLESH

Flesh oh! Flesh, an enemy from the start.

You serve your master, I serve the one who is the keeper of my heart.

You beat me, whip me and cloud my mind.

I can't sleep the same, I'm always on guard with a gun ready to aim.

These tantrums you Pursue, I'm losing my mind.

I turn to the love letters to give me peace of mind.

You try to remove my meat, exposing my bones and telling me I'm the one who is a fake.

Carnal being, how much do you think I can take?

Me by myself, out of my own strength I will lose.

But the one who is Greater, that lives in me,

guides me, it is Him I will always choose.

Every time you plant or drop a bomb, he will and is going to defuse it, no matter what your weapon of choice is, when you go against Him you will always lose.

A BROKEN-HEARTED FRIEND

At that moment I found you, a true friend.

A friend that I can call my sister.

We played together, drank together and laughed together. Back against the back, no one could come against us.

Running a race.

If someone went too fast, we took turns to slow down so we can be at the same pace.

True in true I would die for you even though you didn't ask me to.

Stood by your side, so you didn't stand alone. I told myself when you get close to people, you should be the best person you can be. It's okay to show flaws because they would want me for me.

Love with my all so others can see that there is hope and good people still exists.

I was wrong.

I didn't know love comes with a price. The price is nice but when it doesn't look like it is doesn't mean it won't hurt.

I gave love because I wanted it in return. I am knowledgeable that love is a gift when it is unconditional.

Things changed, and we grew distant.

I had a target on my back that wanted me dead, with fear you fled, didn't care what shot me in the head. Then I finally woke up and saw the hole I was falling in led.

I found my father, and he showed me, love. He taught me how to forgive. He said I was beautiful and my father told me to follow my heart and live.

I'm sorry you felt like I cheated, and became heated with the new relationship that was growing. What you didn't see was my loyalty that I declared and that I was just evolving and flowing.

If you really knew me, you know I would never purposely hurt you. I took a loss, you felt free. You robbed the dream of building a sisterhood from me.

You crushed my love and threw it to be slaughtered.

Did you really care?! Or was it just words spoken? Spending them until you got what you needed.

Then you toss me like an old rag on the ground because I knew the truth of your hidden secrets that cause you to frown.

When you saw me, you had to face the truth because you had bitterness and agony too.

I reached for peace, and you said we're cool, but in public interaction, you ignored me and treated me like a fool. Thinking I did not catch the hidden shade that was leaking through.

All because in your mind I made a covenant with an enemy. Was in denial of the friend that was in me.

Not seeing I was letting the spirit lead me to the ones who were going be by my side, so I did not have to be an actor and lie.

I still have to get on my knees, and plea to release the anger and hurt that is inside of me.

You don't really know how much you hurt me. I just wanted you to take time to listen and put yourself in my shoes and see my heart. That's all I wanted from the start. A real sisterhood.

I cry, my daddy tells me it will be okay because sometimes I want to throw and deliver the pain that I take.

My blood is boiling, the rage rushing through my veins. At that moment it's too late because I have let my old self rise from the grave.
my big brother has to get nailed to the cross again because I just let the sin of wrath activate in my heart within.

I forgive you.

My father gives me an outlet where I can meet you and turn loose all that's in so I won't resent you.

It brings me joy that you're happy now. Living life and embracing discovery.

Even though we have shifted and the bond is broken. My love is always open. I learn to not pour my sugar into coffee that doesn't want to blend.

In the end, don't expect me to launch in motion to pretend.

ATMOSPHERE

Levels move up and down, back and forth.

The presence of the force field can go north, south, east, and west. Walking around wondering if I am at my best.

I am, a part of me says yes. The other part of me says no.

This internal bloodshed between spirit and flesh, I gotta go.

The vulnerability is easy and hard to hide. Don't be fooled by the smile because there is anger and hurt inside.

You guys tell me to be myself, but once I release these feelings, I am the one who becomes the villain.

In a place with a struggle not knowing how to be.

Should I laugh, talk, be quite a or pretend?

If I don't make a move, I will offend.

Honestly, I don't care about fitting in.

There are pieces of some particles in me that wants to, but that region of the world is not real or true.

Everybody is trying to be different

Guess what!!? I am different

I won't try to fight it!

No matter what direction I am going, I'm always invited.

IT

It takes me to a place of high.

It makes me feel alive.

The way it makes me feel golden and clear,

The way it makes me wish and yearn for it to be near.

The way it makes me smile and bring me warmth.

It touches my heart and my skin.

All it makes me wanna do is take it all day all night, every day and every night.

Then it makes me feel empty, a dagger close to my heart. It makes me feel alone in the dark.

It breaks me and cracks me inside.

All it makes me wonder is why?

WINTER

Outside I'm warm, and I believe inside I'm ice.

It scares me,

I am always wondering if I am going to slip and fall into the dark abyss.

Every okay, every smile, and every yes to move along. There are times I believe no matter where I am at or going to be, I'm still stumbling through the same song. My scars of the past are fading as I feel the new scars sinking in.

This torture of being trapped and then being free is hell for me.

Everyone is pushing and strolling, so hell is not their destination. Here, now, I'm living in it. It is driving me insane and giving me frustration.

Every day I prepare for war because behind the doors I do not know what is in store.

I open up my windows to breathe and receive a bliss of laughter. Then storms and fires come in and bring disaster.

How can I let this happen, again and again?

Do you see now? The struggle within.

Ice is beautiful; it's full of love and light. It is also hard and sharp, a shield and a sword to fight. My heart is big and open, it is a lot to bare.

I don't understand why I am like this. My lovely father made me this way.

Sometimes I want to deny it because I am not always pleasurable to be around. I can literally turn a smile into a frown.

It doesn't matter because it works in reverse too. There are times when I feel like I am a quick fix, just like the snow.

The snow glistens, it makes you stand still to listen. Then the snow can freeze you cold all day and all night. Blowing the wind of honesty, leaving you with frostbite.

In the blink of an eye, it's over, they don't want to be in its presence anymore.

My lovely father created me like this, and I still don't know why. I do love Him and trust Him, and that is all the reason I need to try.

He is my lifeline, and he understands me.

His masterpiece is marvelous, I adore it with no doubt.

I am ice, that is what it appears to be.

In the end, he is the one who knows and sees.

DWELLING

I'm feeling last

Keep going to the past

Need to be in the present

Time to let go of the old scent

Make life a joyful blast

IDENTITY

Hello! Who are you?

Oh, do you not know or are you just confused?

Are your anger from your past or are you hurt?

Maybe you are worried because you are always ahead. If you are worried, I will slow down because at any time you can be dead.

Hmmm...... Are you pride?

Too mighty to ask for help because no one understands you. You being like that is bad for your health.

Are you trust? That is a fine asset. Trust is the way to be.

You live in the moment, not caring about what is coming.

You embrace the past without letting it define you.

Embrace all of who you are. If this means you are one or all of the four, don't sink and dive because accepting them will lead you to five.

TUG-A-WAR

You growl at me so I can let go

Creating fear in me to coward out.

My stomach twist, turns and knots are forming.

My brain is screaming, and my heart is jumping out of my chest.

I'm barely hanging on

You laugh and taunt me. Telling me to give up because I had already lost.

I look down and see that I am about to fall.

The doubt rapidly moving in

Posing my mind to let go.

At that moment I remembered that

You are the hoax.

A mock-up that whispers counterfeits and lies.

I am chosen by Him, the Most High

I have the authority over you by calling out to the Heavens.

Back off! Hear my battle cry.

43

In this fight, I am the one who will win and survive.

Awaken

I killed you, and you still try to rise beneath the surface.

If I had not taken the time to forget, you would disappear.

I walk to your gravestone and grieve.

I should never be ashamed, I was you.

Now, we are not the same.

Goodbye.

RUNNING

I'm chasing after you, wanting you more and more.

Without you, I have no identity.

I want to be your humble servant.

I need you! You make me alive

I reach my hand up to you. You reach your hand down to me.

I love you and want you by my side

You bring me joy when I looked at your beauty.

Thank you for your heart, you are my humble servant.

I live in you and will never forsake you.

I want to give you more and more.

I will keep chasing after you.

FLAME

I seek your everlasting love.

Craving to dwell in your presence forever and ever.

I invite you in and let you take control.

My tongue dances to call your name.

I get drunk off your spirit.

I'm never letting go.

Others think I'm an addict.

I am addicted to you.

They just don't know.

The world tells them you are a dictator, but I know who you really are.

A humble ruler who is ready to sweep someone off their feet, when they
come your way.

I had one taste and threw you the key to my lock.

I can't get enough!

I know I have to share you and I'm okay with that.

47

If we all had you, this world would be a better place.

My sweet, beautiful everything I love you.

You will always be the eternal flame in my heart.

Spring the Peace

My identity is that I am a child of God. I found myself through him and his love. He lives in me and told me about my purpose. He loves me for me, and I love myself. Before I didn't accept all of who I was. Also, I carried the chains and shackles of my past. Letting it affect my present. My past is my testimony on how I got here. The present is the new stories and decisions I will make currently. I have a choice, and I will choose for myself. This is my story of my life, and I'm living it. No man or evil can take that from me. My journey is not over, and I'm learning myself every day. That's the best part about the discovery. You are constantly evolving. The difference is, now I have contentment, peace and everlasting love and that I have a wonderful father who is mindful of me. I am His princess. If God is for you, nothing and no one can be against you.

Discovery is an identity found.

HARMONY

The flower opens, and her winter coat has fallen.

She is ready to stretch her steam and roots.

The birds sing, and the butterflies dance.

The flower move in stillness,

Gliding in her garden of approval.

She knows who she is,

A princess of the King.

THE GIFT

Sitting and thinking about where to go.

The heat is smothering the outside air, can the wind blow.

A familiar stranger approaches, offering me wisdom to eat and love to drink.

I'm restored, and patience becomes my friend.

You always surprise me, I have to say,

Answering my need and sending it my way,

Oh my God, you bless me every day.

EMOTIONS

Volcanic ash and rock is the exterior.

Creamy hot passion on the inside.

Being controlled by the pressure of the core.

Erupting or dormant?

When active it's easy to burn the life around.

Inactive the lava is quite, not achieving its purpose.

With balance there is greatness, forging.

LIMITLESS

The galaxy is infinite, so is the source.

Stars tell a story

Constellations are connecting like neurons in the brain.

Organisms are the life on a planet

Floating space dust roaming in its targeted destination.

The perception is all in the eyes.

PAIN

Pain I no longer feel, I'm healed.

Acceptance I accepted into my bosom.

Ingenious stories I love to create.

Nevertheless, always more. I know my worth

MY WISDOM

When I found you, I pictured myself walking through two big brown doors.

Seeing tall wooden shelves that almost touched the glass ceiling

You being so welcoming is a wonderful grand gesture.

My toes wiggle and my hands lay on my lips while I gasp, with excitement.

The fresh vanilla, cinnamon, and coffee aroma you deliver into my nostrils are inviting.

I want to stay in your chambers forever.

You have many aisles that I want to explore.

I get lost being with you.

You make time stand still, that I forget that there is life outside your doors.

Your pages I want to seek.

I love how your words penetrate me.

The books, articles, hymns, and stories sink in.

I desire more.

There is a lot of information you have to share. I can only take in so much.

Every time I come back to visit, you consistently blow my mind.

When I have to leave, I take you wherever I go.

You prevent me from making a simple or complicated mistake.

You cause me to think about what path I should take.

I miss you!!

I can not wait until I am back in your corridors.

I adore how you are in my reach

I am always ready to learn and let you teach.

TRUTH

Truth is sharp like a two-edged sword I let it pierce me.

Reality I took into consideration because it was time to stop running from it.

Uniqueness I took as my weapon, this is who I am.

Tenacious I let go, losing it brought me patience.

Hope is what I keep, my number one tool for survival

THE GOLDEN GLASS

In today's eyes, you would rather be the polish Golden cup that you see.

Not caring or giving a concern with the filth that is inside of me.

As long as I pass with the other cups on the shelf.

I took this, I used this and welded in my soul.

Every time purity will pour into me,

it became Polluted. I'm sick and Disgusted with what I am.

I don't want this anymore.

Hands take me and cleanse me. So when I fall, the smut is around me but not in me.

I would rather be judged with low, being uncontaminated and living; than be judged with the high fake replica, with death manifesting inside.

Dirt is the real beauty, it's where I came from.

The craft maker blew his breath into me, and I am a great creation.

THE BLACK SAPPHIRE

My beauty is enticing, I will enchant you with my breath.

I sparkle in the moonlight, and you see an angelic being.

Do not be fooled by my delicate petals.

I am hard and strong like a rock. Ready to pierce anyone who offends me.

The ebony silk within my skin tells me that I am a true queen.

Embracing the gift and image that God has given me.

Brown sugar and spice and everything nice. This is all of me.

A rare jewel to behold, a rare jewel who cannot be sold.

EVOLVING

Petals all around, petals to the ground.

Shedding layers of your skin.

New beginnings come forth with change.

If the appearance is strange,

You are in the right range

Change is part of the process.

It is hard to let go, and it's scary not to know what is ahead.

Move freely.

Let your fire flow &

Your water spread.

Let your wind blow &

Your earthiness be a homestead.

All is well, well is all.

RAINDROPS

Raindrops hit the streets.

Raindrops on a window pane.

Raindrops fall and cleanse the pain.

Raindrops wash the past, so it doesn't stain.

Raindrops flood out this place to rebuild a new frame.

Raindrops pour inside to fill up.

Raindrops continue to be more than enough.

Raindrops don't ever stop.

Raindrops resume to drop.

IN THE BLOOM

In the bloom, I will be in soon.

Exposing myself in the noon,

To be in tune.

Wrapped in full abundance, I am made new,

While I continue to drink this holy brew.

I'm growing roots and vines,

My enemies know not to cross this line.

I am protected by the divine.

Osha, osha ba ba ba hallelujah!

I praise in my room. Living in his limitless and

In the bloom.

MY BEAUTY

My beauty is not being perfect.

My beauty is enjoying my kinky hair.

My beauty is loving where I come from.

My beauty is embracing and rocking my curves.

My beauty is finding myself.

My beauty is not knowing all the pieces.

My beauty is acceptance.

I AM

I am the bird that soars in the sky.

The bear who is courageous and the protector.

A bee that pollinates the garden.

I am the sunflower that is loyal to its roots.

The dolphin who brings wisdom and peace.

I am the tree planted and firm in the ground, ready to withstand any commotion.

I am of these things and more.

A daughter, sister, a friend and a lover.

I am a child of God, His worshiper, and his server.

Mostly, spirit, soul, water, and fire.

I am set apart with all and with all I am set together.

I am his invention.

Made in the USA
Columbia, SC
11 September 2024

41507847R00039